S0-ACP-763

ALSO BY MARTHA RONK

BOOKS
Desire in LA
State of Mind
Eyetrouble
Displeasures of the Table (memoir)
Why/Why Not

CHAPBOOKS
Emblems
Quotidian
Prepositional

COLLABORATIONS
Allegories (with artist Tom Wudl)
Desert Geometries (with artist Don Suggs)

IN A LANDSCAPE OF HAVING TO REPEAT

IN A LANDSCAPE OF HAVING TO REPEAT

MARTHA RONK

OMNIDAWN   RICHMOND, CALIFORNIA   2004

Richmond, California

www.omnidawn.com

(800) 792-4957

Copyright © 2004 by Martha Ronk, all rights reserved
Printed in the United States of America on acid-free recycled paper

ISBN 1-890650-17-X

Cover: Still from the 16 mm film *Fog Line* (Larry Gottheim, 1970)
Cover design by Quemadura

Cataloging-in-Publication Data appear at the end of the book

CONTENTS

The everyday is what we cannot but aspire to,
since it appears to us as lost to us.

STANLEY CAVELL
In Quest of the Ordinary

I. IN A LANDSCAPE OF HAVING TO REPEAT

IN A LANDSCAPE OF HAVING TO REPEAT

In a landscape of having to repeat.
Noticing that she does, that he does and so on.
The underlying cause is as absent as rain.
Yet one remembers rain even in its absence and an attendant quiet.
If illusion descends or the very word you've been looking for.
He remembers looking at the photograph,
green and gray squares, undefined.
How perfectly ordinary someone says looking at the same thing or
I'd like to get to the bottom of that one.

When it is raining it is raining for all time and then it isn't
and when she looked at him, as he remembers it, the landscape
    moved closer
than ever and she did and now he can hardly remember what it
    was like.

A PHOTOGRAPH OF A PLATE GLASS WINDOW

We come to know ourselves through these photographs
as if they were memories yet to come.
An act of mortification looking at the boy in his arms
not the essay about the light off the plate glass (the bird flying into it)
not learning to keep quiet.
The face out there is the one I used to walk by the store
near where I lived. The items in the window, the curtains I'd
    forgotten.
The boy in his arms was a boy.
The way one no longer has anything to say looking at (the bird flying
    into it).
The wings expand, we say, the wings are expanded in a blue light.
He writes an essay about it and disappears into the future
of photography where the boy used to lie in his arms.

A MEMORY THAT ISN'T YOURS

When the moths fell out of my eyes it was not
the upturned wine glass from the night before
but girls taking communion for the first time.
Holy Ghosts waited around to taste their cool mouths
and run tongues under their milky teeth.
It troubles my sleep where the great bird died.
He says I miss you and I am taken in,
suspicious of the smell it makes all over.
We decide not to go for allegory but to let them.
Skin pulled tight isn't the usual thing but what
carries us beyond sleep and the falling out of my eyes.
You are childless and on the brink of waking up.
What we see is a coastline of different birds,
a memory that isn't yours but just a line
across the horizon. She's kneeling in a pew
and choking up. She'd like to go back and
invent even the smell of it all over again.

SUPERIMPOSITION

It's a real thing.
Even myopia and that craning of the neck.
That putting words in someone else's mouth like wafers.
That deciding how the other must feel
and the image showing up directly on the screen.
The quick glance into it rendered her speechless.
She was to begin with.
After a time there was no one out there to talk to.
Just an echo of what one thought moments before.
The repeated notes of the insistent bird.

Kneel down, move your lips in prayer and you will believe.
Pascal projecting his voice into the void.

The film they watched was a film in which a narrator superimposed a narrative of action seen but from a point of view outside the events so that as a member of the audience one was drawn in and distanced at the same time so that projection was seen as the imposition of the director.

WHAT'S OBVIOUS

The moth moving like a page turning into the next idea
sounds like eating itself.
Who sees the placement of each stone,
the thread winding a morning glory along a tree branch,
a Japanese garden with rearranged stems,
petals shaken on a newly swept lawn.
Who hears the oboe in what isn't even the major movement
or remembers who sat by chance across from
a lost decision, Elgar dropping out of view.

YOU COULDN'T READ A BOOK ABOUT IT

When he goes upstairs he can't find the one he wants
and says, you always like the really depressing ones.
Over time words like *florid* lose their meanings
and the part of the white bird that isn't white is throbbing since
    yesterday
whether I like it or not.
You couldn't read a book about it or take binoculars
as you keep meaning to or use the painting of the crow
this morning over the newly mown hay or was it wheat you saw,
despite the heavy brush strokes, move wings in that slow way.

IN THE HOUSE

She'd like to unbutton the blouse.
She'd like to give up rhetoric but seems unable
and likes adjectives besides.
She'd like to walk to the house for example up the walkway
but the blouse is another story, a second story,
one she'd rather forget.
How are they so certain.
That's it I guess.
How to unloose the tag end
or make a decision different from the usual.
She keeps looking for a migraine in the near future
shimmering its usual pinks and greens.
It's probably yours in the second story bedroom she says.
These days I don't sleep at all she agrees.
Her blouses are usually unbuttoned and how
can she stand it or what about touching all the
clothes in the closet as if they belonged to you.

TRYING

When I raise my arm I do not usually try to raise it.

WITTGENSTEIN

Trying to find out what one thinks is approximate
at best, trying on one thing and then another
or trying to think of what to say
as in *up the Oregon coast or in a fine spray of mist.*
Trying is not something anyone can do, he says
so we go for a walk in the fog as it happens
a coincidence not to do with trying.
The morning's simply overcast for the third day in a row.
Anyone can add the blue of the distant sea.
Anyone can color in the sky.
But the expanse of gray extends beyond what else there is to say.

SOME BIRDS

Life's approximate is how someone might put it
and I think that's sort of true.
It's the monotone moved from one tree to another just a bit further
    down the road.
I sort of study birds he says, I too had a life in the years before
and then there were more years added and it just seemed to go on.
Migration takes some from the far north to the coast of Mexico
    before they begin again.
Their wings are narrower, their tails forked
but the note from the tree I've never heard it before.

AFTER ALL

After all is where one ends up unrepentant because what else is
   there to do.
Well I just got here and what I see after all that has come before
and some coincidental reading is some tree in the next yard.
Or he maundered about badly in the middle of the country and
   did it everyday
until he was finished with the middle of the country and it was
   time to move on.
Still it might have made all the difference in the world.
Something exact might have happened and brought to a finish
   all that had been said and done.
After all it wasn't as if it were a matter of choosing to do it his way.
After all this he says you can still say that to me.

ASKING A PLAIN QUESTION

Why is she knocking at the door she knows no one's home.
She knows the conversation will be approximately the same
but there's no avoiding it which makes it altogether worse.
Only by walking in and with a breezy air asking a plain question
of someone who knows the answer so it's a safe bet.
Sometimes *what time is it* works well and sometimes not.
Sometimes one wants to recognize the various pieces in their
    various places
and sometimes she says in that way of hers, *go find it yourself.*

THE APPROXIMATE FORM OF BEAUTY

The approximate form of beauty was where we stood looking out
at the beautiful view.

Backing off is the only way.

But I like it too much one of them said.

The approximate time is 11:42 and your time is up.

The relative motion of two objects moved.

Proximity is neither *like* nor *not like*.

A camellia in a glass bowl like the one yesterday.

Who's to say this is like that or I like it or taking it in.

I write to you as an approximation of intimacy.

Doesn't one want to move out over the edge.

You taste like grass, he said.

It was precisely 2:45.

A quarter of an hour becomes an arc, a repeated habit, the fixity of
fixed ideas.

How odd to have had the thought, I'm going to have a splendid time.

CLOSER TO MY NATURAL VOICE

I keep a lot to myself although as you say
I am always giving pointed answers to pointed questions
what other kinds are there you say I said what's kept
is a kind of where I was yesterday for example
or a certain whine as I am quoting
although it seems otherwise than it might
but closer to my natural voice as you say isn't
a crucial event but the actual words which I've kept for
such an occasion when what I've kept to myself
as if anyone would want to hear for any reason
except you sound so like yourself again.

THE GLASS PORTRAIT

And maybe I'm the enemy,
could we suppose so, then
the unsettled sink and mantelpiece
would make sense, the nervous
shoes and unbuttoning yesterday's
shirt out there where I was
standing in the mown-down place
supposing I were, would it explain
the sudden and exalted
voice, the stamina of it
muscle tone and what the skin
did, yesterday in the malty
taste under the breastbone, the
opening of the front, my standing
in the place above it, rows
of glass gotten there by logic
or the rim of salt, one tongue
maybe she says you
aren't like that, the purposeful
placement you lie through it
the three fragile ones
lined up, that's all.

A CONVERSATION REPEATED FROM YESTERDAY

Shapeless fog meets the shapeless trees
in an articulation of wires outwitting fog.
We haven't words for it we recognize as our own voices
though he is saying something probably true about the misplaced
    doors
the tilt of dormers and walls.
They would sound insincere coming from our mouths these days.
How to get in past suspicion,
past the flattened leaf flattened on the road we drove on.
It's not as if we mumble or give it a leg to stand on.
There's no giving up irony by getting past the usual signs.

(DONNE, MEDITATION IV)

The function of mere sound,
canary one and canary two,
a stifling bit before the serve-up
consumed with a handful of dust
and it's walking cemeteries again
and eighteen dogs in one solitary sluice
but it hasn't rained despite the blue procession
of a stand of rangy ones what are they
uncertainly wavering in the sound of
a coming they said on the radio
storm perhaps by afternoon or so
there's dance music on in my distraction
of more-or-less centerfold, mindquirk,
cemeteries one and cemeteries two,
what bit of haze in the ear were you
looking for, eyes left and in a tis-true
sort of scatter, sunk so low,
apologetic to the universe writ large
who'd even devote a momentary cry when
even a dog knows his grass recovers him.

AFTER WATCHING JULES ET JIM

The water keeps lifting over the watery weeds.
Without a thought in the world is what we say about the things of
    this world.
Meantime and meanwhile I can't help it.
What is it with these enigmatic smiles
and have you tried that on anyone else.
Also what works in one place doesn't necessarily work in another.
The water keeps lifting over the weeds as the weeks go by.
Now it is today and then it was the film we were watching in French
and her maddening but enigmatic smile.
We walk mindlessly through the weedy water
though the ending of the film was far more dramatic than that.

    *The line which ought to be a line between the sea and sky obscures
        itself badly.*
    It's a messy job but someone has to do it.
    *If one wants things in place, a girl who's beautiful and good
    it's no good watching French films.*

A RUIN THAT ISN'T A RUIN

Also nothing's to be seen inside a random sound.

Or birds screwing around in the trees early morning before they
  repeat.

I guess I wanted to say think of the ending as if we had come
  upon a ruin

that isn't a ruin but we built it as inadvertently as we walked out
  or in.

Or I wanted to say remember her running down the walkway in
  the video before she was a child.

Emulsion, a milky film, a deposit on the side of history.

Yet the light off the side of the building isn't anything more than
how fervently we had thought to do it.

THE DAY WITH MUSICAL ACCOMPANIMENTS

The ordinary day, what a day.
Then adding an overlay of clarinet: the *rainy*, *noisy*, *perfectly*, etc.
Whose voice is in the kitchen
whose body is turning over and moaning in her sleep.
A reflex reaction and next to it
tropological as in characterized by tropes.
All figurative language in the figure.
Her figure reminds me.
It sits in the background and scolds.
A figure admired as only a figure can be.
Only in an ordinary day can one decide the right thing to do
or even any thing at all.

All oboe players are tall and obsessively thin, reedy, caring for reeds
wafting in the streams of music, green as reeds, striped as reeds,
   unnecessarily conscientious.

THE STACK OF WHITE DISHES

It seems the stack of white dishes is enough.
Or ought to be and gathering force.
She's already tried to rearrange her set of beliefs and sexual
    preferences
and moral certitudes and is it that one gets tired
or the real world does its thing
or language just up and shoots off its mouth despite what one
    thinks.
And Debussy is near by and why not.
Helpless in the face of it all
all the things in the places they mean to be in even tomorrow
one might call it fog out there stacking itself against the trees.

PHOTOGRAPHY LOVES BANAL OBJECTS

Being away being more vivid than not.
The object moved out of its usual location revised as a critical essay
was lying on the floor of the room you sit in.
She was sitting with him; she was sitting apart.
If any one thing is moved even inches from its place
the entire composition is ruined.
Who can find it when you do that.
She was as lost as a newsreel from another era.
We live as much in another time as with those of our own.
It was an amoebic shape in turquoise blue;
it was a still life of polished flowers and fruit.
The headlines are illegible at this distance away.
She arranged a bunch of objects end to end and said stay put why
    don't you.

PHOTOGRAPHY LOVES BANAL OBJECTS

The words remained the same despite the variation in scale
manipulated by the program she was using for graphic design
of how much she wanted to tell her.
How much I want to tell you she said.
Use bold for the very bold.
On the other hand reminds me of taking an object
and moving it from left to right
as if a juggler had entered the room and stood where I was standing.
The object is about the same size and could fit in a shoe.
A bird in the hand, even the left hand
fluttering one's skin as nesting objects do.

A PHOTOGRAPHIC COLLAGE (HANNAH HOCH)

An afternoon wasn't enough to fool anybody
nor the breath she remembers breathing.
But later it seemed ridiculous.
Who can get over a grand piano in the clouds
or the group assembled near the top in evening wear
waiting for a breeze to dampen the shine.
No one's ever seen the sound they hear
blind as the fraying moon.
Hers wore smaller feet for the dance.
Of course they're fairly isolated from the world she thinks
who used to think of herself as convivial.

DEFINING OBJECTS

Aside from objects, what holds us in place,
which Byzantine velvet and damask cloth,
what instant camera or pile of books on top of
a photo of *The Angel at the Sepulchre*, Julia Margaret Cameron.
A few minutes ago, sun in the blue haze of humidity
you'd think impossible to hold like the tacked-on gauze
pulling away from museum walls.
I think to anchor mistakenly.
The mosquito scab on the left side, the moth thrown out of the
     sheets.
The further-out moon is one a Virgin might stand on,
her pointed leather shoes like no other shoes today.

HENRY JAMES IN THE FOG

Her body can be perceived through clothes if one wants it.
The white transparency of fog is too romantically cinched
    at the waist
tied with a velvet bow. He was felled he says by a velvet
    bow. (*James*)
There is no place in this flesh that does not see us. (*Rilke*)
    Getting them off isn't for him
he wants to talk it out piecemeal. If the pear rots before he
    snaps a frame,
the day over before he finds a word. He had never let it sink
    in before.
The too obvious burns at his ribs,
twists a rubber band tight over a finger, makes it impossible
    to swallow.

AN AFTERNOON CLOUD OR
LOVE IN THE AFTERNOON

To think you can walk through it
like trying to paint skin.
We sat at the side of the bed our feet on the ground.
Later less like a sea and yet.
We hurry our minds as if we could.
Plausible sounds like its very shape.
Discipline its opposite when we think so.
Yet lesser than the sea and closer.
The skin on her face waited for sunset.
To think ahead of tides
isn't an everyday thing.

DISINTEGRATION (BIO/AUTOBIO):
FOR EVA HESSE

1. KNOTTING THE ENDS

Compulsive winding, bandaging
or what am I worth
and also why don't you leave me alone when I am doing these
    things?
Tying up loose ends here she wrote
picking threads from the floor and knotting the ends.
Two days of working on some dumb thing she wrote
and unable to pin-point belief.
She was always doing it in white and knotting the ends.

The tacked on quality makes them seem the same.

There is a hint of circular motion from which fingers protrude.

Why can't you just leave me alone.
Or what am I worth she wrote.

2. THE CONDITIONS

If the first version is a humble and flexible form
the symbolism is obvious.
Where were you when I was approximately out of my fucking mind.
Graceful is the ability to bend as trees do.
It expands across a room in great calm.
If one uses the language of another as an approximation of one's own.
What she found on the street was a clearer version of how to do it.
What's a conditional phrase.
What's a fish out of water.
What am I doing here and so forth.
If you mean approximately what you say.
The surfaces have a detached presence.
I wish the wind would stop blowing.

Others working in the same medium found the conditions unbearable.

Her condition continued to deteriorate despite knowing how to proceed.

For all of Hesse's determined testing and experimentation with materials she knew latex was not a permanent substance. Sans I, Sans III, and Stratum have, at this writing less than seven years later, already disintegrated.

LUCY LIPPARD, Eva Hesse

3. SANS/ FOG

It seems to stand between touch and the absence of touch
to soften at its hardest edge and melt at the point of greatest definition
marking a grid of liquid between the deck at my feet (clear, vivid)
and the trees in the distance (blurry, gone)
the substance of trying to think about the material substance of the
    material world

—it was made by laying cheesecloth on plastic—

holding the squares of air through the metal grommets stuck into latex
as the branches hold what one faces in place.

It would, of course, be a mistake to see Hesse as consciously anthro-pomorphizing her work. She took great pains to erase such refer-ences. [Yet there is] a profound identification between the artist and her materials, her forms.

4. FETISH FOG FOR EVA HESSE

a.

Fetishes lying under the bed with the sheets dragging on the floor.
No blau sky. How about if it could go and come at the same time
pulling tighter with cords.

b.

I can't figure out how to figure out how to do it.
I figure it'll take a lifetime of complete misery.
Yet she threads a cord through a bit of hosing and it seems
a plausible answer to the questions.

c.

A slap of white across the tabletop could be the cloth for dinner
could be the rectangle of light reflected from the window
could be the open book from which I was reading
could be something akin to a hand coming down hard.

d.

One cup calmly. And later with a hose.

One coffee with milk. And later with a hose.

One coffee with calm white milk to go. And later.

e.

My skin is raw. The metaphor is absent.

One can't see the point of a disposition.

When she pokes grommets through the latex you can almost
    feel them

from off the page and from Berlin which isn't a metaphor either.

5. REPETITION #19 (1967)

Overlapping the edges of clay onto the curve of the container
the large ones are in addition secretive.
I work only in my corner.

in this container I'd put that year when I couldn't stand it

Wouldn't a discovery of material (latex/ rubber) change
the direction of the work entirely.
A rubbing, a drawing, a bit of ribbing in the corner.

it was the year I found it by accident

They've lost their syrupy surface and have darkened to
a deep brown. This is a color I'd like to avoid.
She said she liked crawling because of disintegration.

the other year to choose would be the one before the last

Other tendencies were held in abeyance or remembered later.
It's painted on in layers as it ages. As you can tell from the rings
that repeat themselves around the edge.

intensity turns out to accumulate years day by day

It is a kinetic use of materials almost like a house.
Two working drawings have worked me into the corner.
They are roughly sewed into the bedroom upstairs.

also the year her mother died

Secretly she always meant to. It was a work in progress.
As though it could take whatever life had in store. The bins
    were lined up.
The basic unit seemed to be solid tubing.

how many more months left to do it

6. DISINTEGRATION OF MATERIALS

disintegration of materials frustration of working to work

with someone else   to work out how to   keep the frame

of reference to keep from   disintegrating

into an idea   an idea   whose idea is one becoming

one's own work   what is it this work of one's own

who worked it out   losing a standpoint from which to put forth

one's own   work is it   is it one's own

who moved   of materials in the workspace

provided for   forever, lose, panic   it's yours

anticipated what you were   =to say subtitled in a text

materials, chemistry, surface, pressure, self, automatic, shy

discovering in the time between   after you'd already said it

historical sense   non-work   nothing of one's self

test studies for the one you work with

II. IN THE VICINITY

1. HOME MOVIES

In the home movies the girls run around the magnolia tree, the small one planted in the exact center of the lawn. In Ohio then, design meant the *exact center* or *in a row or all alike*. They are wearing the same dresses with the same navy blue coats and the same shoes. They have the same haircuts with bangs like Scout in *To Kill a Mockingbird* except that one is blond. I am the tallest. I am always the tallest and it is all up to me. During nap time I fly around near the ceiling, hovering, imagining lands mapped in blue ink. The film flickers and dies. When one opens her mouth to speak, the silent mouthing breaks my heart. Later they change to everyday clothes, jeans and t-shirts, and run outside and hang upside down from tree branches. The blinding sun breaks through the screen of crab apple blossoms when the wind blows. The film burns.

2. SCREENS AND TOOTHBRUSHES

The screens were framed in wood; the toothbrushes were old ones brought from home. The children collected maple leaves and pinned them at exact angles on white paper. I especially liked splatter painting with blue paint because there are no blue leaves. The leaf in outline on the white paper was white. The autumn leaves were yellow or red. Entire afternoons were spent in such time-consuming art projects and time was endless and radiantly boring, like looking through the screen to another world in which not only is reality brought down to size, framed and recolored, but also time itself: I would never go home, always be suspended in the back and forth motion of the brush across the screen, always bumping my knees on the underside of the same school desk.

3. CEDAR POINT

There were always holes in the screens. *Ha, ha*, my father said, *gotcha*. The junebugs got in as we wiped the sand from between our toes. These were the days which seem as idyllic as pastoral and as incomplete. In the dream I played on the blue rug with a child who is no longer a child. The father is furious so the child tells me to be very quiet. We are as surreptitious as possible and crawl about on all fours until we get to the screen door where he catches us by the bands of our jeans. *Aha*, he says. The insects we called junebugs were airy and their wings fell off in transparent heaps, so delicate the screens destroyed them utterly.

4. SCREEN MEMORY

The movie screen obliterates memory. We are lost in the eternal present.

The indifferent memories of childhood owe their existence to a process of displacement: they are substitutes, in [mnemic] reproduction, for other impressions which are really significant. The memory of these significant impressions can be developed out of the indifferent ones by means of psychical analysis, but a resistance prevents them from being directly reproduced. As the indifferent memories owe their preservation not to their own content but to an associative relation between their content and another which is repressed, they have some claim to be called 'screen memories.'

SIGMUND FREUD, *The Psychopathology of Everyday Life*

5. NEAR THE EDUCATIONAL INSTITUTION

I am walking barefoot in the snow. This is after I can't think how I will manage to lecture to the large auditorium when all I have prepared is a few notes for a few scholars in a small conference room. So I drink too much coffee and decide to walk to clear my mind. Having never left the institution before, I am immediately lost in a strange neighborhood I've never seen before and my feet are icy cold. The neighbors from whom I ask directions have no idea what I am talking about. They know of no educational institution in the vicinity.

Finally, someone offers to walk me there. The doors are barred shut so I crawl in a basement window over the tops of summer screens, bicycles, ladders, garden hoses, rakes, all painted the same blue. It is precarious but I am a gifted climber and I use my toes. I take the same elevator I always take to the fifth floor. The halls smell of gravy and meat and the iron doors clang before the elevator crawls upwards. Upstairs I try to find my dorm room. My roommate whom I don't meet until many years later is always on the east coast making a movie and is never in her twin bed next to mine. My lecture notes are never on the desk, in my briefcase, or in the pockets of my jeans.

6. IN THE VICINITY OF THE MALL

In Florida the TV is always on a game show. Everything is bright: the grass beyond the porch screen, the TV screen itself, Vanna's teeth. I walk to the strip mall to get my nails done but the beauty businesses are closed on Mondays so I go to the Americana store and buy miniatures: a wire basket with tiny bottles of milk, a tiny Santa in his sleigh, a broom and dust pan the size of a thumb. The past shrunk up and packaged in shrink wrap. I read that men are especially suspicious of nostalgia because it means home. The contestants on *Jeopardy* know a little bit about a lot of things and think they are getting somewhere. I'd like to buy an "a" says the woman wearing the requisite blue.

7. NEAR WHERE I HAD ONCE LIVED

At the pool in Florida the men talked of their illnesses and grand-children; they counted my laps. One had a toenail turned black and about to fall off. One had changed doctors on the advice of his neighbor. One had a can of beer and a preferred route to Chattanooga. Some of the streets in the dream are in an Ohio neighborhood where I had once lived so at least I knew to ask for the cross street, but I never got to that street or the one where our house was but wandered about slowly as if under water. I wandered out of a hospital into a celebration of the Day of the Dead and knew myself to be near where I had once lived, but I could never find the house. When I ask the Mexican women standing with their crow masks and baskets and children how to get home, they stare at me as if I were speaking too slowly. The men at the pool were "snowbirds" and they talked of getting their cars ready and just shutting the door and taking off.

8. MOVING

And then you have caused yourself to be missing from the cardboard occasion in which we were wrapping up numerous boxes and sliding lid slot into lid slot. Where shall we go after that, and after that.

I remember being taught how to tie up packing twine: make a loop, insert the free end into the loop and pull tight around the box of books as you leave the place you have lived in, painted the floors, folded the sheets, cooked the soup, kissed the man you will never see again. You take down the bricks and boards, put the books into boxes and leave. You are always leaving and eating. You are one of the fortunate. This time you have a place to leave from, to go to.

9. ON THE ROAD

In the novel there is often a carriage. Sometimes Sherlock is riding along stoned out of his mind. Sometimes the countess is on her way to a dinner party. In both cases someone is usually dead by the end of the evening. I, however, have only lost my bearings. I am lost again in the nearby vicinity of my very own home. I try to remember things by putting an opened and twisted paperclip over the steering wheel—the jagged edge is to remind me of things. I still forget to buy gas.

Then I run out of gas on the freeway and think that I will die walking in the rain down the onramp toward the pizza hut but I only get soaking wet. The guy behind the counter tells me a bad joke, but I am polite and laugh because the AAA man has arrived and soon I'll be on my way to the dinner party and besides I can never figure out how it is that Dr Watson is the only one who knows how stoned Sherlock is and who laughs at his jokes. For my own part I am glad for the novel because one has to live somewhere other than on the freeway.

10. IN THE VICINITY OF THE 7-11

The novel has its eye on the past in which one character of a particular station and class says something to another character of a particular station and class, all decked out in tie-dye and nose rings, hiphuggers thrust towards the 7-Eleven and the hypercorrected politeness of the Sikh who sells lottery tickets with a smirk and whose daughter is on the floor behind the counter clutching an Alice in Wonderland doll.

The girl with the orange t-shirt wants an orange pop, the Edenic desires for bubbles popping in the mouth, the color orange which may or may not have been the first shade she tried on at the MAC counter before she slipped it in her purse.

11. THE DOCTOR'S OFFICE

I have myself pierced, small studs in my mouth and behind my ears. I taste silver with my tongue. On the radio the film director says one must never turn one's eyes away. When I finally convince the woman who is my dream stand-in to remove the small thin nails, her body is covered in sores. I lie down on the blanket in the doctor's office and pour disinfectant on the wounds, but I am in the wrong office and the bodies are interrupted in the midst of some sort of sexual encounter on my bed for which I apologize and sign up for more.

12. VENICE

Later, in the vicinity of Venice her skin was pock-marked with
the saint's acid sores, a fantasy she thought you're thinking of
Ursula and like the blue glass beads he'd bought for his wife she
stood holding them knowing they were for someone she'd never
met and would never know her name and she'd picked them out
nonetheless and stood in the expensive glass shop holding them
and running them between her fingers as if she lived in London
which was where she thought he was from. It was his home. She
wanted to hold him in her arms. Afterwards, they went to see the
series on Saint Ursula at the Academia and she had a reason to
cry.

13. BOLOGNA

Near the center of Bologna I stood in the hot sun smelling old stone. Not pungent, only vaguely of urine. It was so hot no one seemed able to move except in the somnolent manner of old dogs, gray at the muzzle and leaning into the ground. She told me hers had arthritis and had to be fed a special macrobiotic diet which she cooked for him every night and fed him alfalfa pills which I should also take and give up hot dogs and potato chips and she spoke in Spanish, a language I don't know. I had come to Bologna to look for the Morandi paintings I knew had to do with sex though there'd be no way to explain this since they are so formal, so cool, so much, anyone can see, about the formal arrangements of color and shape.

Nonetheless I was certain of my point. More to the point, I was lost again and how was I to find the museum which was, I knew, located in the vicinity of the cathedral, although since I couldn't speak the language I couldn't ask anyone, when all at once it was hotter than before and it was now high noon and the bells began to ring.

14. THE RIVER IN AZUZA

At the center of the dream in the center of the picture frame was a stroke. However, it wasn't a stroke he died from. No one knows yet what it was, nor what really affected the girl who claimed she had rabies from a cat bite. She had no teeth marks on her arm, not even small ones.

The monks practiced and practiced with the ink brush until the stroke was perfect. It was their life. The pole of bamboo, the pole of a rod. On one glazed bowl the stroke is so perfect it drips into the shape of a long-legged bird, the symbol for longevity. After the autopsy what will they know except grief and the loss of someone who went fishing in the river in Azuza only to fall in and make the other fisherman laugh.

15. NEAR CHINATOWN

I know someone who says that expensive LA restaurants are filled with the homeless. On the other side of the copper screen the diners at their white tablecloths look as if they are in Casablanca. On my side is the bar which the present owner got from Yee Mee Lou's. I spent early years in this town, *this stinking town* as Chandler would say, drinking blue drinks at that bar; they gave off vapors like dry ice and hangovers. I sat for hours having conversations with a thin man I didn't meet for several years after the bar closed. We talked about trips we would take, porches we had sat on, books we meant to read. When he drew his long finger over a picture in one of the books, I knew I would never leave LA.

16. IN A SUMMER VILLA

A man of twenty-four has preserved the following picture from his fifth year. He is sitting in the garden of a summer villa, on a small chair beside his aunt, who is trying to teach him the letters of the alphabet. He is in difficulties over the difference between "m" and "n" and he asks his aunt to tell him how to know one from the other. His aunt points out to him that the "m" has a whole piece more than the "n"—the third stroke.

FREUD, *The Psychopathology of Everyday Life*

17. NEAR THE ART GALLERY

If what is in the frame is a session with a shrink, one can only come to know what one knows. This being especially difficult if also so obviously simple. However, if one doesn't have the frame, it is nearly impossible, which is why photography is so important in this century. Without it and without the grease pencil to mark the crop lines, who would be able tell. Near the plate glass windows near the art gallery, I saw a man walking about aimlessly. He went hither and thither. He held his fingers in a rectangle in front of his eyes and thereby came to know what he knew.

18. IN THE MUSEUM OF ASIAN ART

If one draws a line such that it has a momentum of its own or re-calls or echoes some phrase, refers to a set progression of some sort and then interrupts or overlaps it or sets it athwart, the erotic might be brought to mind.

I was standing next to her at the museum in front of a painting of mountains to which the monks had been banished for reasons lost to the mists of time. We are, I said to her, in relation to one an-other. I know where I am only in relation.

Ezra Pound's example: *the pine tree in the mist upon the far hill looks like a fragment of Japanese armour.*

Her sweater was purple as I recall and mine pink, neither one either here or there, although the mountains in the painted were highly tinted by the setting sun. Too much is random these days, she said, tossing her sweater over her shoulders and smiling her unfathomable smile.

19.

The vulture phantasy of Leonardo still absorbs our interest. In words which only too plainly allude to a sexual act ("and has many times struck against my lips with his tail"), Leonardo emphasizes the intensity of the erotic relations between the mother and the child ...W. Pater, who sees in the picture the embodiment of the entire erotic experience of modern man, discourses excellently on 'that unfathomable smile always with a touch of something sinister in it.'

FREUD, *Leonardo da Vinci*

20. NEAR MUIR WOODS

The two girls are mine though I have no girls and we are all lost in the maze of a large city in which buses run at right angles. I can see us from above in a bird's eye view scurrying along and trying to find our way. I am in charge but I have no idea where we are. Dizzy and anxious, I wake in a sweat. Our house must be somewhere in this city, but the girls are crying and I am holding their hands and beyond the city, situated at the top of the map, is a mythic forest with scrubby pines where I keep trying not to go.

They get separated from me in the center of town near a large department store at the corner of streets whose names I realize are the names of other things. Still, I look for them in the noodle shops in the basement. They are wearing white starched pinafores I tell the policeman who is out of an early movie comedy fat and Irish and directing traffic with oversized white gloves. Kim Novak is walking, impossibly, in a white coat and white gloves and white heels in Muir woods among the trees reading the labels on a fallen Sequoia: here, she says, is where I was born and here I died.

21. NEW HAVEN

I wander the streets, brick and concrete and cobblestone. It is a dreary sort of day or towards evening and I am rushing along, late to get somewhere, when he passes me, the man now long dead, and although he is on the other side of the street and at a distance, I having rushed past and he at a distance, I recognize him in my skin, these dreams the most uncanny I have because the disembodied is so clearly sensed in the way in waking life with one's back turned, one knows the person one loves has come into the room.

I chase after him, but as always he moves implacably forward, steady, slow, heavy in his movements and large as he was, wearing his tweed coat, a coat he continued to wear as his life came undone, and I am unable to catch up to him despite his slow and methodic movements.

Sometimes he disappears into a building with gothic rooms, sometimes into bars where I push through a crowd of men who know him, who swear they know him, if not exactly where he might be at this moment.

Then begins the trial of phone calls, trying to contact those who know him, trying places I know he once lived, trying to reach relatives who have inevitably moved, trying to open address books which won't stay open, trying to locate the number. Then when I have a ghostly number in front of me, trying to get the phone to work and trying to place a call to ask where are you I am lost and have to come home.

22. THE DOGS AND CHURCHES IN
MY NEIGHBORHOOD

When I am out walking in order to be at home in my own skin is what I say to people who ask why I am walking when I could drive or else I say to get warm when they know LA is never cold, I come across dogs. The dogs have been chained up usually because the ones on the loose frighten people and pin them to the street until someone drives by in a car to rescue them. So they are chained up and you can hear them growling and rattling their chains unless you are in Echo Park where the dogs are never chained.

Others are going to the evangelical church on the corner because it is replaced by the used car lot which was there long before the church and has now returned. They are not Orthodox but they seem to be required to walk nevertheless because they are always walking in groups larger than twos or threes. *God is love* is what the church spells out for us in large letters on a bulletin board behind glass. Sometimes, *Welcome to the house of God.*

23. HOMESICK

One can, oddly, best conceive of home, the most private perhaps of spaces, by going out into public ones, although in most western cities there are few public and social spaces to be had, only the lonely road. One is at home on the road, in a trailer, a mobile home, a mobile phone, a home on the range without fences or ties that bind or apron strings. Home it turns out is more often elsewhere than not. Most Americans are vaguely homesick, traveling the highways or airways.

24. GETTING HOME AND INTO BED

Miraculously, after the game or concert or fireworks display, thousands of fans find their cars (no matter that they are all white or black or Hondas or Nissans) with the orange Garfields stuck to the rear windows, start up, merge lines of impossible traffic in acres of parking lot, head for the freeways (101, 5, 405, 2, 210 etc.), drive thousands of tons of metal bearing wives and husbands and children and dogs all wearing their proper seatbelts, and find a house and open the garage door with a garage door opener that opens their particular garage door and take off their various Ts with various logos and without feeling a bit lost, fall into bed on various sheets (flowered, striped, satin, flannel, dotted and lace) next to some other person without thinking who is this in my house, how did he, she, I get here after all.

25. OUR HOUSE

Since his home was a wreck he took pictures of houses. Since books were disappearing, he began to dream of them. Since we had met long ago, we began to meet again. Since the subjects looked similar, we assumed they were. Since we look alike, everyone supposes we are. Since my eyes are failing, the print is getting smaller. Since the photographs of houses were small enough, they fit into a file folder. Since he was moving, it was more convenient. Since he wanted to paint the house blue, I insisted on gray. Since the camera broke, he bought a house. Since the pictures turned out blurry, he looked intently. Since doubles are a frequent occurrence in modern art, we cut our hair. Since we both like to read, we embraced an identical house. When I looked in the hallway mirror, the triangular one in carved blond wood my mother had coveted and spent too much for, I noticed that my image was missing. She stood there instead. When he noticed it as well, we were, as they say, in somewhat of a jam, though from an analysis of consequences, it was erotically interesting and modestly discrete.

26.

On the evening of the dream-day the dreamer had been in a book-shop, and as he was waiting to be attended to he had looked at some pictures which were on view there and which represented subjects similar in the dream.

FREUD, *Interpretation of Dreams*

27. WHERE YOU LIVE

When you click on the remote the whole picture comes alive,
disappears, comes back, disappears, and history is a present mo-
ment in which we float. The team wins, it is World War II, Myrna
Loy ruffles her blouse, whole populations are displaced, Judy
Garland sings and the ice woman from Siberia lives, dug up by
the French anthropologist and translated for PBS. You can see
yourself, you are almost moving into the house you always
wanted to live in. It is all exactly the same only more so. You are
living with a sister, a husband, a fellow camper, a lover, a friend of
a friend of a friend. Your mother is sitting on the stairs in the old
house humming something and disappearing. She says, you
won't remember this and it's lost, but we filmed every scene
twice to be sure we got it—in the home movies there you are in
your new Easter dresses, running around the tree and then run-
ning around it again just to make sure.

28. THE SCREEN IN THE LIVING ROOM

When the TV is on, color invades the living room. When the game is on everyone roots for the team everyone is rooting for. You can't help it. There is no more out-of-doors except for the underprivileged who are forced to play in the streets, turn on fire hydrants, play stoop ball, spray graffiti names across stucco walls: *loco, loco, loco.* The TV is now the sole source of the sublime, invading and blocking, offering up all the material goods one can imagine and keeping them safely at an arm's distance away. Always blocked, the sublime turns a deaf ear, turns a face to the wall, rises up like Mt Blanc which is now merely a pen writing in blue ink and completely out of date except for the expense.

29. MORE SCREENS

Each intimate gesture was a parlor game of sorts. They threw pillows across the room and never turned off the screens. One screen squiggles colors of the rainbow in shapes reminiscent of '60s drug paraphernalia. A peacock appears on the patio, on NBC, in the dreams she has of once having had sex. No one, she remembers he said, *has sex*, it's the wrong way of saying it.

The two Italian women, each beautiful in her own particular way, one dark, one blond, jumped on the bed together and threw feathers at each other, giggling. According to the interpretation in next day's paper it was a ritual of sorts. Her breasts jiggled. Her wig flew off. The peacock flies from roof to roof highlighting the day. Men in spandex run across bright green astroturf, their bottoms firm under the elastic fibers, heads hard as their helmets.

Flannery O'Connor kept peacocks in the yard; she said they talked to her in screams like her innermost thoughts. I too was afraid and worse knew no philosophy.

30. A TV INTERVIEW

What did you have in mind he said the Buddhist from Tibet said. Cut the body centimeter by centimeter from top to toe and where do you find the soul. He was photographing the body in extremes of agony, penile implants, open heart surgery, cataracts. There is no black hole where the iris sits. It is no longer necessary to go anywhere which is no longer different from anywhere else.

31. E-MAIL

Date: Mon, 5 Feb 1997 09:26:58-0800
From: Chinesescholar@univ.edu
To:
Subject: cinnabar

Cinnabar was the renown elixir of ancient China. When taken in properly prepared dosages—lots—it was to provide euphoric states of life and, more importantly, immortality among the gods in the afterlife. Emperors sought it above all else; the most powerful of these—Ch'in Shih Huang Ti—lived and died on it alone. The irony of this diet of the gods is that red mercuric sulfide is, like all mercury, toxic in extreme degree: the afterlife being so excellent, cinnabar will rush you there.

32. E-MAIL

Date: Tue, 6 Feb 1999 09:26:58:0800
Subject: the usual corner

Meet me on the usual corner, if you're not there by 5 I'll know
you can't make it or I'll stop by the Clearwater and see if you're at
the bar. If not, I'll "mosey" on. Did you ever have that experience
of standing to wait for someone and think you see them [sic] and
they are ever so familiar and then the person turns around and
the faces [sic] you saw on the other side of the hair is completely
different and for a split second one face is superimposed on top
of the other. Probably not. Nonetheless,
I look forward to seeing you one day at home. yrs.,

33. HOME MOVIES

I can see my face in the screen, also the picture on the wall behind me. I might live over my shoulder in that room before I turn the computer on, but afterwards everything is in front of me, at the next magnification, the next Mandelbrot, the next future of a memory that replays a swing set that used to talk back in a voice that sounded vaguely familiar. Someone croons out of my mouth when I wash the dishes. Someone is a constant scold and over my shoulder. Someone is writing down the story of my life; on the radio he's singing a Mellow Yellow you wish you didn't remember. I heard the author say in a TV interview, when you get to be as old as I am the past is more vivid than today and you can play it all back in slow motion and take yourself through the same wallpapered rooms looking at your parent's wedding photograph again and again and again.

34. UNHEIMLICH

We find things uncanny when they are familiar yet also somehow foreign. Those things which remind us of beliefs that we may have had as infants, or of primitive beliefs which our society has long abandoned. Thus it is that heimlich and unheimlich can actually be synonyms.

FREUD

It was always very familiar to me finally.

After a time I recognized it right away.

In the midst of all uncertainty, her assurance was unwelcome.

The face seems familiar but only when turned to the wall.

I was virtually alone.

Someone who looked similar stood next to her and so she took
their picture.

I believed I'd see him again but always at such a distance I could
never be sure.

The child painted the windows of the houses like eyes in a
rectangular face.

Once the sun went down, the ones on the hillside had the same
sort.

I pressed the home button on the keypad again and again.

III. QUOTIDIAN

You look familiar to me he says.
What can one say about what is familiar and why what
    seemed so at first
turns out to be inconsolable?

❖

We say it looks familiar but not my face and not
looking where one thinks to see it
and not in the window passing quickly by.

❖

The recording of everything.
The broken wire,
the dead thing on the drive,
the number of minutes of sunlight on record for this date.

❖

Birds and coffee. What can indefinite mean.
He says ritual has taken over history.
It has altered anything we might think to say.

❖

The gesture looks familiar.
He kisses her arm.
And the unrealized friction and the coming storm
and the driving back for twenty years.

❖

While he was doing this, I was doing that.
During the same time, within a range of, at some distance from.
Or he says a word such as *assumedly*.

❖

And then he said aren't you mad this time and I said
it isn't the same. Is it ever and if not how can one compare.
Betrayal is the one walking one foot after another after what you did.

❖

Must the events of the day disappear
in order to be daily.
I don't notice the sky, my voice isn't sharp.
Again, you're obligingly gone.

❖

In a dream I see our house open to the elements
and you ask me to lie down on the bed
while two men merge and stand by the door waiting.

❖

In the midst the hum, the drip, the slight air.
The itch on a forearm, the burn on the tongue.
Yet a list isn't it and especially not the dream of her cutting my hair.

❖

In the jumble of everyday: Japanese beetles, silver spoons and
     another box to fill.
The leaves are frayed, the clothes damp,
the compost, the eggshells, the nails in an empty can.

❖

Therefore he was always unsure what to do.
Once I knew a man who had no idea what to put on.
I walked into his arms because I was uninvited and he knew it.

❖

Who can help hoping there's something else up
before we arrive to pack the boxes.
It was in a sequence he explained all along.

❖

The perfect stranger seems so long ago that one picks up a glass
    not liking champagne.
The allium's in bloom.
He says everyone you could live with is boring.

❖

One day was entirely my mother cutting my hair.
It had been at night under closed eyes
and straight across the forehead as before.

❖

I keep thinking it must be solid as if what I thought about
    didn't count.
Then I thought about how I had spent the day trying to
    read about dissolution
and how it had taken the whole day.

❖

The moth's copper wings tick.
It's as if one could pick them up between finger and thumb.
There's a postcard from Shanghai in the box.
In his hands, now mine.

❖

There are now noises I don't want to hear.
I think instead of the man who taught me to tie boxes
and of things that are useful.

❖

The too familiar is a pungent incursion.
Touching is another kind.
All summer waiting for our arms and legs.

❖

How perfectly ordinary expresses an attitude.
About the edges of the books a sort of dampish curl.
Objects have no thoughts about anything else.

❖

The leaves float to the bottom of the bedsheet.
Where was I last night I can't get out of.
Trying to remember is of no avail nor my mother.

❖

Everyday something comes around.
To come down off one's high horse.
When the dress was thrown over her head afterwards.

❖

The mother is cutting the hair straight across the forehead.
The forehead is damp as if a wash cloth has been pulled
across it, as if a towel lay across her lap.

❖

In the time it takes it's almost over.
Not exactly forgiving.
How one hates packing and unpacking books.
When she left she took nothing with her.

❖

I dreamed of being licked across my eyelids.
The man I recognized was familiar in other ways.
One time he stood in the sunlight glinting off his glasses.

❖

No one speaks of it exactly as I would.
The feel of his fingernails under my hand.
That his hands smell of butter,
unresisting as one could only have been at the time.

❖

When the air cools my skin grows expectant
as if the door would slam
as if the row of heads would turn to the side to see what's there
as if she cut off my hair.

❖

Those things one doesn't have to notice or notice much.
No interruption on the way to them.
That you are not lying next to me is related
to newspaper ink on my hands.

❖

There is the plan and too strident a color.
I heave something majestically into view.
A desire for the drama of woe.

❖

Off the smokey red dress the edges burn.
The other wishes it were as quiet as before
one smooth bowl next to the other.

❖

Intuition leaks from the corner.
The only plan is sleeping for as many hours as possible
seeing you at least in profile.

❖

I saw my mother cutting my hair.
She says they come here of their own accord,
you can't keep them out even if you want to.

❖

The way he looks in the dark unlike his chest after running.
Water still comes down when the wind blows.
Sometimes the click of the wooden door.

❖

He says it's humid after the rain and stands over me in his jeans
pulling off a damp shirt.
In the novel he throws off the top sheet in the heat of his dream.

❖

Moreover the days lengthen and it's twilight far longer.
winding up the ball of twine with the circular motions.
Around and around takes a long time.

❖

In the morning I can't get up.
Light travels in slanted rays across the wall.
I watch it, heavy, dispirited
between sink and stove.

❖

When the wooden door taps itself shut.
When the winds blow high in the trees.
When my own motives are held by the chair inching into the sun.

❖

Whether it can be let in in any form or name.
Or must it make a low hum.
First an elbow, finally a fact.
Forgetting, the hardest part.

ACKNOWLEDGMENTS

Special thanks to Omnidawn Press for extraordinary care and thoughtfulness. Thanks also to the Djerassi Artist Residency where many poems in section one were written, and especially to Cris Bruch for discussions about Eva Hesse. "A Photograph of a Plate Glass Window" is for Jacob Lifson. For the "Quotidian" poems, thanks to Diane Ward.

Poems in earlier versions:

"Quotidian" selections: *Quotidian*, a chapbook (a+bend books, 2000); *Fence* (Spring/Summer, 2001).

"It's like a landscape," "A Photograph of a plate glass window," "History of a marriage": *108* issue 91 (2001), ed. John Lowther.

"Disintegration for Eva Hesse": *Conjunctions* web magazine, 2001.

"Superimposition," "Photography loves banal objects (Being Away)," "The day with musical accompaniments," "Henry James in the fog," "In the House": *Aufgabe* 2 (2002).

"Closer to my natural voice," "Photography loves banal objects (by Minor White)," "An afternoon cloud or love in the afternoon": *Jubilat* 5 (2002).

"In the Vicinity" 27–32: *Pool* (2002).

"The stack of white dishes": *CutBank* 59 (Spring 2003).

"You couldn't read a book about it," "Defining objects," "The approximate form of beauty": *Slope* 17 (Winter/Spring 2003).

"Donne: Meditation IV," "A memory that isn't yours": *Colorado Review* 30:2 (Summer 2003).

"Photography loves banal objects (The words)": *No: a journal of the arts* (2003).

ABOUT THE AUTHOR

Martha Ronk is the author of several books of poetry, most recently *Why/Why Not* (University of California Press). She is also the author of a memoir, *Displeasures of the Table* (Sun & Moon). Her chapbooks include *Prepositional* (Seeing Eye Books) and *Quotidian* (a+bend books). Her collaborations include *Allegories* (Italy: ML&NLF) with the artist Tom Wudl and *Desert Geometries* (Littoral Books) with the artist Don Suggs. Her fiction and poetry have appeared in many journals including *Chicago Review*, *Harvard Review*, *The Denver Quarterly*, and *Hambone*. Her awards include the Graham L. Sterling Faculty Award for Excellence granted by Occidental College, a MacArthur Research Grant, and residencies at MacDowell and Djerassi. She is the Irma & Jay Price Professor of English at Occidental College and co-poetry editor for *The New Review of Literature*.

Library of Congress Cataloging-in-Publication Data

Ronk, Martha Clare.
    In a landscape of having to repeat : poetry / by Martha Ronk.
        p. cm.
    ISBN 1-890650-17-x (pbk. : alk. paper)
    I. Title.
    PS3568.O57415 2004
    811´.54--dc22
                                                2004011416